COMPUTER SOFTWARE CATALOGING
Techniques and Examples

DEANNE HOLZBERLEIN

T0402622

Routledge
Taylor & Francis Group

LONDON AND NEW YORK

First published in 1986 by The Haworth Press, Inc.

This edition first published in 2020
by Routledge
2 Park Square, Milton Park, Abingdon, Oxon OX14 4RN

and by Routledge
52 Vanderbilt Avenue, New York, NY 10017

Routledge is an imprint of the Taylor & Francis Group, an informa business

British Library Cataloguing in Publication Data
A catalogue record for this book is available from the British Library

ISBN: 978-0-367-34616-4 (Set)
ISBN: 978-0-429-34352-0 (Set) (ebk)
ISBN: 978-0-367-42302-5 (Volume 19) (hbk)
ISBN: 978-0-367-42303-2 (Volume 19) (pbk)
ISBN: 978-0-367-82337-5 (Volume 19) (ebk)

Publisher's Note
The publisher has gone to great lengths to ensure the quality of this reprint but points out that some imperfections in the original copies may be apparent.

Disclaimer
The publisher has made every effort to trace copyright holders and would welcome correspondence from those they have been unable to trace.

Computer Software Cataloging: Techniques and Examples

Deanne Holzberlein

The Haworth Press
New York • London

Computer Software Cataloging Techniques and Examples has also been published as *Cataloging & Classification Quarterly*, Volume 6, Number 2, Winter 1985/86.

The Haworth Press, Inc., 28 East 22 Street, New York, NY 10010-6194
EUROSPAN/Haworth, 3 Henrietta Street, London WC2E 8LU England

Library of Congress Cataloging-in-Publication Data

Holzberlein, Deanne.
    Computer software cataloging techniques and examples.

    "Has also been published as Cataloging & classification quarterly, volume 6, number 2, winter 1985/86"—T.p. verso.
    Bibliography: p.
    Includes index.
    1. Cataloging of computer programs. 2. Cataloging of computer programs—Specimens. 3. Descriptive cataloging—Rules. 4. Anglo-American cataloging rules. I. Title.
Z692.C65H64   1986   025.3'49   85-27221
ISBN 0-86656-477-2

Computer Software Cataloging Techniques and Examples

Cataloging & Classification Quarterly
Volume 6, Number 2

CONTENTS

Introduction

Library catalogers call computer software "machine-readable data files," and then define these as computer programs designed to be inserted and run on a computer. The computer software being discussed is for microcomputers only. Catalogers do not include as "machine-readable data files" (or mrdf) the single purpose gameboards with built in programs. Thus, for a cataloger, a hand-held calculator, computer football game, or a programmed chess or checkers set would not be considered a "machine-readable data file."

The examples and discussion presented here conform to: *Anglo-American Cataloguing Rules,* 2nd ed., 1978, supplemented by: *Guidelines for Using AACR2 Chapter 9 for Cataloging Microcomputer Software,* 1984, and *Cataloging Service Bulletin,* and should assist catalogers in producing accurate records for national data bases, such as OCLC, RLIN, UTLAS, WLN, etc.

Following the business-oriented software are suggested simplifications, consistent with these rules, to assist catalogers who do not plan to store records on a national data base. When the simplified records follow the *Guidelines* for the main body, then the information on the simplified records can be used later to retrieve full cataloging records from a network. If simplified records are too brief, a later need for full bibliographic detail can mean recataloging the material.

TITLE SCREEN = CHIEF SOURCE OF INFORMATION

The chief source of information is usually the title screen, the information seen on a cathode ray tube soon after the program begins. The *Guidelines* say it may be: "a part of the program's description, or as part of the listing of the program and its statements.'' If the title is not located on the screen soon after the program begins, is not found in a printed listing of the code, is not found as a part of the program's description, then the following are used in the order given here:

1. the [original] label on the disk, cassette, or other storage device,
2. the [original] label on the container (box, etc.),
3. the accompanying documentation, or
4. other published descriptions, such as reviews. (Advertising descriptions should not be used.)

It is the original label on the disk that is used for cataloging.

AREAS AND THEIR SOURCES OF INFORMATION

The following areas use the following sources for their wording:

Title/statement of responsibility	Title screen is ''chief source''

Edition
Place, publisher, date
Physical description
Series
	Title screen, or
	   Label on disk, etc., or
	   Label on container, or
	   Accompanying documentation.

File description Notes ISBN	Any source

If a title screen is not available, the title is taken from the following, and in this order "of preference":

1. the label on the software;
2. the label on the collection as a whole, such as a box;
3. accompanying documentation, such as guides, manuals, etc.; or
4. published descriptions.

"Accompanying documentation" does not refer to documentation for the file itself, nor does "published descriptions" refer to advertising information. When the title and statement of responsibility do not come from the title screen, they are placed in square brackets, according to AACR2, 1.1A2. An example of this is seen in *[VisiCalc]*.

As can be seen from "Areas and Their Sources of Information" given above, the edition, place, publisher, date, physical description, and series may come from any source that would normally be part of a computer package, and need not be bracketed. Some disks will not have a main title screen, but will have a menu or directory. Disks with a menu instead of a main title screen occasionally have title screens for the individual programs. As standards are developed for "machine-readable data files", there will be more collective titles and title screens on the commercial disks, but there will always be variations with the "locally produced" software packages.

TITLE AND STATEMENT OF RESPONSIBILITY

The cataloger gives the author and title information in the following form:

Title [machine-readable data file] : other title information / statement of responsibility.

All the information outside the brackets comes from the "chief source of information", which is generally the title screen. The wording is copied from the title screen, the punctuation and capitalization follows "prescribed" AACR2 forms, given briefly in 1.1B1, and the order follows that stated in the first sentence of this paragraph. Thus the words must come from the chief source, but the order may be transposed for the catalog entry. The title screen may begin with the author's name, or presentor's name, and unless this is inseparable from the title, it is moved to the statement of responsibility area. *Story Machine* is an example of the transposition of an author's name to the statement of responsibility area. An example of an inseparable title is *Commodore 64 Logo,* where the title may be *Logo,* but cannot be realistically separated from the beginning words: Commodore 64. For these situations, an added title tracing is given for this other title.

NO COLLECTIVE TITLE

When there is no collective title, then the software is cataloged according to the rules for material lacking a collective title, that is, according to 1.1G1 and 1.1G2. When one work is dominant (see AACR2 1.1G1), the catalog record is the same as for any other single title with added contents, such as *Technology* in this work. It is when no work is predominant that the form changes slightly, and this is shown in the example, *Resist V.*

EDITION

As described in AACR2 1.2B3, the words used in this area can include: edition, issue, version, etc. "Version" is the current microcomputer term employed to represent updates to programs, and catalogers need to search for this, and it may be given as V.1.1, or occasionally, just: 1.1. The number to the left of the period indicates the major edition number, and the number to the right indicates the minor revision number to the specified major edition. Thus the term of "version" implies relationship to the internal programming of the software. A version statement is shown in *Heatloss* and *Chem lab simulations*.

Educational and business computer software generally use edition to indicate either the brand of computer the program will run on or the group of people the program was written for. Popular programs have been re-written or edited to run on Apple, Commodore, Atari, IBM-PCs and other computers, and so will use the edition statement to indicate, say, the Commodore version of this program. An example of this is in *Bank Street Writer*, where this work shows the Commodore 64 version of a program available also for the Apple computers. At other times, edition statements may hide within them a reference to advanced, regular and beginning users. An example of this is *Cause and Effect*.

PLACE, PUBLISHER, DATE

The place lists the city, and the state, with the state abbreviated according to Appendix B of AACR2. If the zip code abbreviation is given on the item, then, and only then can the zip code abbreviation be used. The address of the "publisher" may be supplied in parentheses, and this is frequently added when no ISBN number is given. If there is a publisher and a distributer, then both are given, and no address is supplied.

The publisher's name is given in brief, but clearly understandable terms.

The copyright date to be put in this location is the date on the software program. If the date on the manual, guide, or program differs by two years or more, this fact can be added in the notes.

PHYSICAL DESCRIPTION

The extent of the item is given in terms of the number of files and either:

     data file
     program file.

Program file is the more general, and is used in all cases of doubt whether it is a program file or data file. Data file is the more specific, and is used when this information is given on the material being cataloged. When the number of files is known, the number is given. When the number is not known, "ca." (an abbreviation for the Latin "circa", meaning about) is given, without brackets by the number listed. Following this is a parenthetical expression giving the language the program was written in, a comma, and the name of the computer system the program runs on. However, the name of the computer system is given in the physical description when the program runs on ONE AND ONLY ONE MAKE AND MODEL OF COMPUTER. Otherwise, this information is included as a part of Note 15, system requirements. Finally, the medium is given; computer disk, cartridge or cassette. A cataloger may consider the disk or cassette has one program file on it when there is no definite indication to the contrary.

Other physical details may include: double sides, sound, color.

The dimensions refer to the computer disk or cassette, and then may add the container for the whole package. The dimensions for the computer disk or cassette are given in inches, with the disk and cartridge given to the nearest 1/4 inch, and nonstandard cassettes to the nearest 1/8 inch. Standard cassettes do not have their dimensions given. (See AACR2 6.5D5 about standard cassettes.) The dimensions for the container are given in the metric measures to the nearest centimeter.

Accompanying material has some restrictions. For material

that meets all the requirements given just below, it is included in the physical description area. Material failing to meet ANY OF THE CRITERIA given below is listed in Note 11.

Criteria for accompanying material:

—the material must be issued at the same time as the computer program;
—the material must be produced by the same company, producer, distributor, etc. as the computer program, AND be by the same author as the computer program, OR make no mention of an author;
—the material must either have a generic title (manual, guide, instructions, etc.), or be dependent upon the title of the computer program, or have the same title as the computer program. In other words the accompanying material must have: same date; same or no specific author; same or generic title. If any of the preceding is not true, then the added material is listed in Note 11, and not as accompanying material.

EXAMPLES:

1 program file on 1 computer disk ; 5 1/4 in. + 1 manual (4 p. ; 29 cm.).

1 program file (Commodore 64) on 2 computer disks : double sides, sd., col. ; 5 1/4 in. in book, 30 cm. + 1 guide (27 p. : ill.; 29 cm.) + 1 set of worksheets/quizzes ([24] p. ; 29 cm.).

1 program file (Commodore 64) on 1 computer cartridge : sd., col. ; 3 in. in box, 23 × 17 × 3 cm.

2 data files, 5 program files (TI-99A) in 1 computer cassette.

SERIES

A series title may be listed on the container, the documentation, or on the title screen. When found, it is added just after the physical description information. Listing a series title for microcomputer software requires the same careful searching of the series authority files as for book series titles. When the cataloger considers the series title worthy of tracing, this tracing adds another title entry by which this software may be found in the catalog. Examples of series titles are given in *Readability Analysis* and *Story Machine*.

NOTES

Notes are given in the same order and with the same punctuation as in the main body, except a period and space is substituted for a period, space, dash, dash, space. See: AACR2 1.7A3. Below are the notes with the MARC information as used in the OCLC system because people have asked to have this information included.

Note 1 Nature and scope.
    OCLC field: 500.
    This note is used only when the title does not convey the content of the material.

Note 2 Language of item.
    OCLC field: 500.
      EXAMPLE: In English and Spanish.
    Information about a programming language belongs in Note 15.

Note 3 Source of title proper.
    OCLC field: 500.
      EXAMPLES:
      Title from disk label.
      Title supplied by cataloger.

Note 4 Variations in title.
    OCLC field: 500.

EXAMPLE:
Title on disk: COT-3 Haiku.

Note 5 Parallel titles.
OCLC field: 500.

Note 6 Statements of responsibility.
OCLC field: 500.
EXAMPLES:
Coordinator, Karen Jostad ; developer, Doris Bower ; programmer, Rick Anderson.
Editors, Marge Kosel, Michael L. Roney ; programmers, Jon Sweedler, Cathy MacMahon.
Producer, Educational Information System ; authors, Joyce and Jerry Adams.
Program, Clark Quinn, Margaret Weinstein ; documentation, Sharmon Hilfinger, Lesley Czechokics.
Commodore version by Frieda Kekkerkerker.

DO NOT include assistants or people who have made only a technical contribution. (From LCRI 7.7B6)

Note 7 Edition and history.
OCLC field: 503.
EXAMPLE:
Based on an earlier module by: Dick Clark, Neal Prachow.
OCLC field: 537. Source of Data. Gives Display constants:
Source of data:

Note 9 Publication, distribution.
OCLC field: 500.

Note 10 File description and physical description.
OCLC field: 500.
EXAMPLE:
Sound can be turned off.

Note 11 Accompanying materials.
If the accompanying material has a different date than the

computer program; or the author(s) of the accompanying material is/are different from the author(s) of the computer program; or the title of the accompanying material is distinct and different from the computer program, then information about the accompanying material goes in this note. The note is used when any one of these conditions is true.
OCLC field: 500.
EXAMPLE:
Booklet entitled: The Ghost of Christmas past (37 p.) / by Dan Stump.

Note 12 Series.
OCLC field: 500.

Note 13 Dissertation.
OCLC field: 502.

Note 14 Audience and restrictions on access.
OCLC field: 521. Has Display constant: Audience:
EXAMPLES:
Audience: For ages 4-12 years.
The cataloger copies the words from the manual.
container, etc. whenever possible.
OCLC field: 506. (restricted use)
EXAMPLE:
Restricted use until 1991.
Copyright until 1990.

Note 15 Mode of use.
Generally, begin this note with the standard phrase: "System requirements:". Give any of the following information in the order listed here, provided it is found on the computer program, accompanying material, or package:

1. "make and model(s) of computer" the program runs on; . . .

2. "memory required"; . . .
3. "operating system"; . . .
4. "software requirements"; . . .
5. "peripherals needed or recommended." *Guidelines* p. 9.
   When possible, give the information as quoted from the
   program or accompanying material.

OCLC field: 538. Technical details note. When needed, type
in: System requirements:

    EXAMPLES:

    System requirements: Apple DOS 3.3.

    System requirements: Apple II (or higher); 48k; DOS
        3.3.

    System requirements: 128K; DOS 3.3; 2 disk drives;
        printer.

    "Runs on VIC 20 and Commodore 64."

Note 17 Summary.

    OCLC field: 520. Summary. Gives Display constants: Sum-
mary:

    EXAMPLES:

    Summary: Game for 2-6 players to reinforce:
        coordinating addition and multiplication; working back-
        words (algebraic reversability); determining the entry
        point to a problem; distinguishing between what must
        be, might be, and can't be; and determining formulas
        from factors, sums, and products.

    Summary: Game 1. A blank face to complete by choosing
        from eyes, ears, noses — Game 2. Make the face wink,
        frown, cry, etc. — Game 3. Repeat winks, frowns, etc.
        To teach programming, keyboard skills and concentra-
        tion.

    Summary: Simulates introductory college level chemistry
        experiments. Demonstrates Hess's Law by having the
        user determine the heats of reaction of three separate
        chemical reactions.

Note 18 Contents.
  OCLC field: 500.
    EXAMPLES:
      Indexes used: Grades 1-3: Wheeler/Smith Index. Spache
        Index. Dale-Chall Word List — Grades 4-Adult: Dale-
        Chall Index. Fog Index. Flesch Grade Level. Smog
        Index.
      Formulas/data from: ASHRAE handbook, 1981 fundamen-
        tals. New York, N.Y.: American Society of Heating,
        Refrigerating and Air-Conditioning Engineers, Inc. —
        Home energy disclosure manual / Rick Anderson, et al.
        St. Paul, Minn. ; Minnesota Energy Agency, 1981.
  OCLC field: 505. 1 Gives Display constants: Contents:
    EXAMPLES:
      Contents: Heat capacity of the calorimeter — Heat of neu-
        tralization of HCl_{ag} and $NaOH_{ag}$ — Heat of solution of
        $HaOH_s$ — Heat of reaction of HCl_{ag} and $NaOH_s$ — Hess'
        Law.
      Contents: Introductory concepts — Prefix tutor — Suffix
        tutor (easy) — Suffix tutor (hard) — Root word tutor—
        Word building — Review game.
  OCLC field: 505. 2 Gives Display constants: Partial contents:
    EXAMPLE:
      Partial contents: Humurabi — Hangman — Hangmath —
        Hello — Hi-Q — Jotto — Le Perdu — Logiblocks —
        Magic square.
  OCLC field: 523. Chronological coverage & dates of data.
    EXAMPLE:
    Block census data for DeSoto, Mo. for 1980.

Note 19 Numbers borne by the item.
  OCLC field: 500.
    EXAMPLES:
    High Technology: 17094.
    Milton Bradley: 7882.
    Sunburst: #1095.

Note 20 Copy-specific note.

OCLC field: 583. Local, copy-specific information.

OCLC field: 590. Local information. This prints only if the institution's profile designates printing it.

Note 21 "With" note.

OCLC field: 500. Linking entry complexity note.

This may change to field: 501, if MARBI gives approval.

TRACINGS

In subject cataloging, the first subject heading is the most specific one, and describes the total program. Catalogers desire the first subject heading and the classification to be the same or similar, although this ideal is not always attainable. The free-floating subdivisions: "Computer programs" and "Computer assisted instruction" may be added to the subject headings.

Added entry tracings may include the name and make of the computer. *PFS File* is an good example covering both subject and added entry tracings.

LOCALLY PRODUCED PROGRAMS

Locally produced programs are usually written or developed locally, and often exist in only a few copies. When considering how to catalog these, and what information needs to come from what sources, one should remember that LCRI 1.4D1 says, "For cataloging purposes, treat privately printed works as published works even if they have been distributed only to a very limited group (e.g., a keepsake for dinner guests or a Christmas greeting for friends). Treat the person or body issuing the item, whether a commercial publisher, a private press, or a person or group for whom it may have been printed, as the publisher." So most microcomputer programs would fall into the category of "published works" when one considers the number of copies and backups that would normally be produced. Thus the source of information for a "locally produced" machine-readable data file is the same as for a commercially produced software. A hypothetical entry is given in this work called *Spelling program.*

ARRANGEMENT OF THIS WORK

Examples of catalog entries for microcomputer software data files are given in this work in three sections: educational software, game software and business-related software. The computer disk label and information from the computer screen is given before each catalog entry. After the catalog entry there are a few explanatory remarks which include references to the *Anglo-American Cataloguing Rules,* 2nd ed. (called here AACR2), and to the Library of Congress Rule Interpretations from the *Cataloging Service Bulletin,* (called here LCRI).

Educational Software—
Elementary and Secondary Level

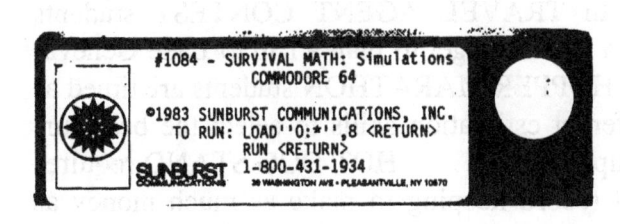
Label

```
SUNBURST
COMMUNICATIONS
COPYRIGHT 1983
```
Screen 1

```
WOULD YOU LIKE TO ADJUST
THE COLOR?   (Y OR N)
```
Screen 2

```
          SUNBURST COMMUNICATIONS, INC.
              SURVIVAL MATH  V.1.0
        BY WALTER KOETKE AND ERIC GRUBBS
  _____

    1)   TRAVEL AGENT CONTEST
    2)   SMART SHOPPER MARATHON
    3)   HOT DOG STAND
    4)   FOREMAN'S ASSISTANT
    5)   DESCRIPTIONS
    6)   END

         Which number? _____
```
Screen 3

Survival math is a set of four computer programs that simulate realistic situations, is designed to motivate students in grades 7-12 to become actively involved in developing their skills in mathematical computation . . . [and] utilizes the computer's ability to randomly generate problems and events. . . . In TRAVEL AGENT CONTEST students work within a given budget to plan a trip to Lake Geneva. In SMART SHOPPER MARATHON students are timed as they use different estimation skills to select the best purchases in a supermarket. . . . HOT DOG STAND requires planning and record keeping to make as much money as possible while managing a hot dog stand. . . . In FOREMAN'S ASSISTANT, the most difficult program, students must be able to convert units of measure, work with area and perimeter, and construct a room from the information provided. Accuracy in calculation is essential.

—from the Introduction
in the Teacher's Support Booklet.

```
Koetke, Walter.
   Survival math [machine-readable data file] / by
Walter Koetke and Eric Grubbs. -- Version 1.0. --
Pleasantville, N.Y. (39 Washington Ave., Pleasant-
ville, NY 10570) : Sunburst Communications, c1983.
   1 program file on 1 computer disk : col. ; 5 1/4
in. in book, 30 cm. + 1 guide (27 p. ; 29 cm.).
   For grades 7-12.                                   Note 14
   System requirements: Commodore 64.                Note 15
   Summary: Randomly generated realistic situations  Note 17
to develop skills in mathematical computation.
                        (Continued on next card)
```

```
Koetke, Walter.
  Survival math [machine-readable data file] ...
c1983. (Card 2).
  Contains: Travel agent content: Work with a budget    Note 18
to plan a trip -- Smart shopper marathon: Timed play
in selecting best purchases in a supermarket -- Hot
dog stand: Planning, record keeping and managing for
profit.-- Foreman's assistant: Work with geometry to
construct a room from given information. Accuracy in
calculation essential.
  Sunburst: #1084.                                       Note 19
  1. Arithmetic--Study and teaching (Secondary)--
Computer programs. 2. Business mathematics--Study
and teaching (Secondary)--Computer programs. 3. Con-
sumer education--Study and teaching (Secondary)--
Computer programs. I. Grubbs, Eric. II. Sunburst
Communications (Firm). III. Commodore 64. IV. Title.
```

Title/statement of responsibility: These were taken from the title screen.

Place, Publisher, date: The address was given because there was no ISBN given. The copyright date was taken from the title screen.

Notes: Note 10 describes the equipment and software needed to run the program. Note 14 gives the age level and came from the teacher's guide. This note is used "only when the information can be quoted from the publication." LCRI 2.7B14. Notes 17 and 18 were taken from p. 2 of the teacher's guide.

Tracings: The second author was traced. The publisher and the computer system were traced.

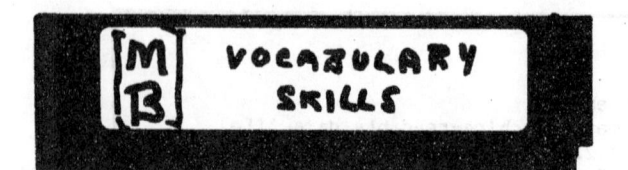

Label

(MB)

Screen 1

(
VOCABULARY SKILLS
   PREFIXES, SUFFIXES, ROOT WORDS
FROM MILTON BRADLEY COMPANY
   (C) 1983   BY MB CO.
   ALL RIGHTS RESERVED
)

Screen 2

(
VOCABULARY SKILLS
   INITIALIZING ....
)

Screen 3

(
VOCABULARY SKILLS
      RUN LESSON
   ENTER   CLASS NUMBER   (1-5)
   AND HIT RETURN: ____
)

Screen 4

```
Vocabulary skills [machine-readable data file] :
   prefixes, suffixes and root words. -- East
   Longmeadow, MA : Milton Bradley Co., c1983.
   1 program file on 1 computer disk ; 5 1/4 in. in
box, 38 x 3 x 24 cm.
   Authors, Contemporary Perspectives, Inc., Robert       Note 6
M. Coldwell, Richard P. Cummins.
   With Microcomputer software guide (36 p.) and a        Note 11
set of worksheets and quizzes (24 p.).
   For upper elementary and junior high grades.           Note 14
   System requirements: Apple II; 48K; DOS 3.3;           Note 15
Applesoft BASIC.
   Contains: Introductory concepts -- Prefix tutor --     Note 18
Suffix tutor (easy) -- Suffix tutor (hard) -- Root
word tutor -- Word building -- Review game.
   MB: 7882.                                              Note 19
   1. Vocabulary--Study and teaching (Elemenatary)--
Computer programs. 2. Language arts--Computer
programs. 3. Word recognition--Study and teaching
(Elementary)--Computer programs. I. Milton Bradley
Company. II. Apple II--Applesoft BASIC--DOS 3.3.
III. Title: Prefixes, suffixes, and root words.
```

Title and statement of responsibility: These came from the title screen.

Place, Publisher, date: The address was given because no ISBN was given. The copyright date was taken from the screen.

Physical description: Since the guide and the worksheets had a different name than the name on the title screen, they were not listed as accompanying material, although they were located in the box.

Notes: Note 14 gives the grade level and came from p. 4 of the guide. This note is used "only when the information can be quoted from the publication." LCRI 2.7B14. Note 15 describes the equipment and software needed to run the program and came from the bottom of the box.

Tracings: Because patrons want programs that will run on "their" particular computer, librarians add the name of the computer the program will run on, followed by the language and operating system, if these are known. Either the language or the operating system or both may be omitted.

Label

$$\Big(\ \text{LOADING, PLEASE WAIT}\ \Big) \qquad \text{Screen 1}$$

$$\Big(\ \text{OK} \quad \text{RUN}\ \Big) \qquad \text{Screen 2}$$

$$\Bigg(\ \begin{array}{l} \text{COMMODORE 64 LOGO} \\ \text{COPYRIGHT (C) 1982, 1983 TERRAPIN, INC.} \\ \text{COPYRIGHT (C) 1981} \qquad \text{MIT} \\ \text{WELCOME TO LOGO!} \end{array}\ \Bigg) \qquad \text{Screen 3}$$

```
Commodore 64 Logo [machine-readable data file]. --
   West Chester, PA : Commodore Business Machines,
   c1982.
   1 program file on 2 computer disks : col. ; 5 1/4
in.
   Commmodore 64 Logo tutorial by Virginia Carter      Note 11
Grammer, E. Paul Goldenberg and Leigh Klotz, Jr. ;
edited by Mark Eckenwiler (ca. 200 p. ; 22 cm.).
   System. requirements: Commodore 64.                 Note 15
   Summary: Interpretative computer language.          Note 17
   1. Logo (Computer program language). I. Commodore
Business Machines. II. Commodore 64. III. Title:
Logo.
```

Title and statement of responsibility: The title came from the title screen, and the copyright owner statement was not taken (and should not be taken) as the same thing as a statement of responsibility.

Place, Publisher, date: The two letter postal abbreviation was given on their published material, so "PA" was given, instead of the normal "Pa." which is taken from page 556 of AACR2.

Physical description: The title of the accompanying paperback book is: *The Commodore 64 Logo tutorial,* written by Virginia Carter Grammer, E. Paul Goldenberg, and Leigh Klotz, Jr.; edited by Mark Eckenwiler, published at the same time and by the same company as the microcomputer software. It was decided the title was not substantially different from the disk, and that the authors would not be traced, so information about the book was given as accompanying material. This book had several numbered sections, rather than one or two numbered sequences, so the total pagination was approximated.

Notes: The age level was not given in the published information so it was not listed in the catalog record.

The title given below will be cataloged as a set because the school owns all five disks. Material is cataloged as a set whenever possible. When the library owns only one part of a set, and the cataloger cannot find an accurate catalog record for the set, then it is necessary for one part of the set to be cataloged as an independent entry, as shown in Elementary. Volume 4.

Label

```
( Microcomputer Workshops
          Presents
    English Achievement I
  Written by Douglas Higgins
          (c) 1982  )
```
Screen 1

Page 1
I will give you part of a sample English
Achievement Exam. Then I will score it,
reporting to you not only your probable
score on a real exam, but also areas for
you to study.
There are sixteen problems. If you wish
to have more, I will oblige at the end of
the first section.
    Press _return_ to continue
    Press _S_ to skip instructions

Screen 2

Directions   Page 2
Each of the sentences has four parts
highlighted and numbered. Only one of
the parts can contain an error. If there
is no error, then type '5' no error. If
you wish to skip a sentence and return to
it later, you may.

Screen 3

MICROCOMPUTER WORKSHOPS COURSEWARE
776 Westchester Ave Port Chester, NY 10573 · (914) 937 5440
© 1980,
Apple Computer, Inc.
ENGLISH ACHIEVEMENT II
48K APPLE

Label

Microcomputer Workshops
Presents
English Achievement II
Written by Douglas Higgins
(c) 1982

Screen 1

        Page 1
I will give you part of a sample English
Achievement Exam.   Then I will score it,
reporting to you not only your probable
score on a real exam, but also areas for
you to study.
There are sixteen problems. If you wish
to have more, I will oblige at the end of
the first section.
    Press return to continue
    Press S to skip instructions

Screen 2

Directions   Page 2
Each of the sentences has four parts
highlighted and numbered. Only one of
the parts can contain an error. If there
is no error, then type '5' no error. If
you wish to skip a sentence and return to
it later, you may.

Screen 3

Label

Microcomputer Workshops
        Presents
   English Achievement III
Written by Douglas Higgins
        (c) 1982

Screen 1

Page 1
I will give you part of a sample English
Achievement Exam. Then I will score it,
reporting to you not only your probable
score on a real exam, but also areas for
you to study.
There are sixteen problems. If you wish
to have more, I will oblige at the end of
the first section.
     Press <u>return</u> to continue
     Press <u>S</u> to skip instructions

Screen 2

Directions   Page 2
Each of the sentences has four parts
<u>highlighted</u> and numbered. Only one of
the parts can contain an error. If there
is no error, then type '5' no error. If
you wish to skip a sentence and return to
it later, you may.

Screen 3

Label

Microcomputer Workshops
Presents
English Achievement IV
Written by Douglas Higgins
(c) 1982

Screen 1

```
        Page 1
I will give you part of a sample English
Achievement Exam.  Then I will score it,
reporting to you not only your probable
score on a real exam, but also areas for
you to study.
There are sixteen problems.  If you wish
to have more, I will oblige at the end of
the first section.
    Press return to continue
    Press S to skip instructions
```

Screen 2

```
Directions      Page 2
Each of the sentences has four parts
highlighted and numbered.  Only one of
the parts can contain an error.  If there
is no error, then type '5' no error.  If
you wish to skip a sentence and return to
it later, you may.
```

Screen 3

ENGLISH ACHIEVEMENT V
48K Apple

© 1980,
Apple Computer, Inc.

MICROCOMPUTER WORKSHOPS 225 WESTCHESTER AVE
PORT CHESTER NY 10573

Label

```
  Microcomputer Workshops
        Presents
   English Achievement V
Written by Douglas Higgins
       (c) 1982
```

Screen 1

```
        Page 1
I will give you part of a sample English
Achievement Exam.  Then I will score it,
reporting to you not only your probable
score on a real exam, but also areas for
you to study.                                    Screen 2
There are sixteen problems.  If you wish
to have more, I will oblige at the end of
the first section.
    Press return to continue
    Press S to skip instructions
```

```
Directions      Page 2
Each of the sentences has four parts
highlighted and numbered.  Only one of
the parts can contain an error.  If there    Screen 3
is no error, then type '5' no error.  If
you wish to skip a sentence and return to
it later, you may.
```

```
Higgins, Douglas
  Microcomputer workshops presents English
achievement [machine-readable data file] / written
by Douglas Higgins. -- Port Chester, NY (225
Westchester Ave., Port Chester, NY 10573) : Micro-
computer Workshops Courseware, c1982.
  5 program files on 5 computer disks ; 5 1/4 in.
+ 5 manuals.
  For grades 10-12.                                    Note 14
  System requirements: Apple II; 48K; DOS 3.3.        Note 15
  Summary: Sample questions from English Achievement  Note 17
Exams. Answers are scored, and areas shown for
further study. "To give students practice in prepar-
ing for the editing format of the CEEB English
Achievement Test."
  1. English Achievement Test--Study and teaching--
Computer programs. 2. English language--Grammar--
Study and teaching--Computer programs. I. Micro-
computer Workshops Courseware (Firm). II. Apple II.
III. Title. IV. Title: English achievement.
```

Title/statement of responsibility: From the title screens.

Place, Publisher, date: The address was given because there was no ISBN given. The copyright date was taken from the title screens.

Notes: Note 14 gives the age level and came from the manual. This note is used "only when the information can be quoted from the publication." LCRI 2.7B14. Note 15 describes the equipment and software needed to run the program and is given in the fullest detail on p. 11 of the guide to number 4. Note 17 was adapted from p. 1 of the manuals.

Tracings: The firm in the publisher field was traced. The computer system is given when the material is for one system.

Label

```
Minnesota
Educational            Elementary
Computing               Volume 4
Consortium             Version 4.2
     COPYRIGHT 1980   TX 472-179
```

Screen 1

```
         ELEMENTARY VOLUME   4
           AVAILABLE PROGRAMS
1. ESTIMATE        5. SOLAR DISTANCE
2. MATH GAME       6. URSA
3. ODELL LAKE      7. END
4. ODELL WOODS
TYPE THE NUMBER OF THE PROGRAM YOU WANT.
(IF YOU WANT DESCRIPTIONS, TYPE 'D'.)
```

Screen 2

ELEMENTARY VOLUME   4
DESCRIPTIONS

ESTIMATE--
  PROVIDES DRILL AND PRACTICE ON ESTIMATION IN
  ADDITION, SUBSTRACTION, MULTIPLICATION,
  DIVISION AND PERCENTS.
MATH GAME--
  PROVIDES DRILL ON THE FOUR BASIC MATHEMATICAL
  OPERATIONS.
ODELL LAKE--
  SIMULATES A FOOD WEB IN ODELL LAKE. THE USER
  TAKES THE ROLE OF A FISH AND TRIES TO SURVIVE.
ODELL WOODS--
  A FOOD WEB SIMULATION INVOLVING ANIMALS FOUND
  IN NORTHERN MINNESOTA.
      PRESS SPACE BAR TO CONTINUE

SOLAR DISTANCE--
  TEACHES CONCEPT OF DISTANCES BY HAVING
  STUDENTS MAKE 'TRIPS' TO PLANETS IN
  DIFFERENT VEHICLES.
URSA--
  A TUTORIAL ON CONSTELLATIONS, INCLUDING A
  SECTION ON HOW TO TELL TIME BY THE STARS.
      PRESS SPACE BAR TO CONTINUE

Elementary. Volume 4 [machine-readable data file] /
Minnesota Educational Computing Consortium. --
Version 4.2. -- Pleasantville, N.Y. (39 Washington
Ave., Pleasantville, NY 71570) : Sunburst
Communications, c1980.
  1 program file on 1 computer disk : col. ; 5 1/4
in. in notebook, 29 cm.
  Revised from: Elementary... my dear computer /   Note 6
Marge Kosel and Geraldine Carlstrom.
  Title on disk and cover of guide (77 p.): Ecology,   Note 11
astronomy and arithmetic.
  For grades 2-6.   Note 14
                          (Continued on next card)

```
Elementary. Volume 4 [machine-readable data file]
   ... c1980. (Card 2).
   System requirements: Apple II; DOS 3.3.              Note 15
   Summary: Estimate: Provides drill and practice in    Note 17
estimation in addition, substraction, multiplication
division and percents -- Math game: Provides drill
on the four basic mathematical operations -- Odell
Lake: Simulates a food web where user takes the role
of a fish and tries to survive -- Odell Woods: Food
web simulation involving animals -- Solar distance:
Gaining concept of distance by trips to planets in
different vehicles -- Ursa: A tutorial on constel-
lations; includes telling time by the stars.
   Sunburst: #995.                                      Note 19
   MECC: TX 472-179.
                        (Continued on next card)
```

```
Elementary. Volume 4 [machine-readable data file]
   ... c1980. (Card 3).
   1. Ecology--Study and teaching (Elementary)--Com-
puter programs. 2. Astronomy--Study and teaching
(Elementary)--Computer programs. 3. Arithmetic--
Study and teaching (Elementary)--Computer programs.
I. Kosel, Marjorie. Elementary my dear computer.
II. Minnesota Educational Computing Consortium. III.
Sunburst Communications (Firm). IV. Apple II--DOS
3.3. V. Title: Ecology, astronomy and arithmetic.
VI. Title: Estimate. VII. Title: Math game. VIII.
Title: Odell Lake. IX. Title: Odell Woods. X. Title:
Solar distance. XI. Title: Ursa.
```

Title/statement of responsibility: See AACR2 1.1B9 for this form for a main title. This is amplified in 12.1B4. This is used when one has only one part of a set. Whenever possible, the set is cataloged as a whole, and the different parts and subparts are given in a note. The title on the disk label and on the cover of the manual is quite different from the title on the screen and the title page of the manual. Both titles should be available to the patron, so one will need to be traced. In order to be traced, indication of this other title is given in a note.

Place, Publisher, date: The address was given because there was no ISBN given. The copyright date was taken from the title screen.

Notes: Note 6 came from p. 1 of the guide. Note 11 gives the name of the program as it was given on the Guide and the disk label. This note is necessary because this title is traced, and everything traced needs to be clearly understood from the catalog record. Note 14 gives the age level and came from pages 3, 10, 16, 30, 46 and 57 of the Guide, where the grade level for each different program is listed. This note is used "only when the information can be quoted from the publication," LCRI 2.7B14. Note 15 describes the system's requirements from p. 77 of the guide. Note 17 was taken from the descriptive screens and from p. 2 of the guide. Note 19 is the publisher's number, and since there have been two publishers, there are two numbers. The number 995 came from the disk label, and TX 472-179 came from the title screen. The numbers are listed separately, according to LCRI 5.7B19, for music cataloging.

Tracings: The Guide, on page 1 acknowledged a debt to a previous work. This was given in a note, so a tracing could be included for this earlier work. The tracing omitted the ellipses in the title. The publisher was traced. The computer system is given for material on one system. The title of each of the six programs was traced because these programs are often requested by patrons, and because these programs are repeated on several MECC disks.

LOCALLY PRODUCED SOFTWARE

Below is a hypothetical program, designed to show cataloging of a locally produced disk. LCRI 1.4D1 (CSB 25) states: "For cataloging purposes, treat privately printed works as published works even if they have been distributed only to a very limited group (e.g., a keepsake for dinner guests or a Christmas greeting for a friend). Treat the person or body issuing the item, whether a commercial publisher, a private press, or a person or group for whom it may have been printed, as the publisher.''

```
Spelling for First Graders                    Locally
                                              produced label


(     Spelling program      )                     Screen 1
   written December 1984
```

That's all the title there is. The cataloger knows this was written by Ms. Smith's 6th grade class at Northland Junior High, in Uptown, Illinois. There is a xerox page of typewritten information which accompanies this disk. There are copies of the disk and xerox copies of the information in the first grade classroom, the computer lab, and the media center. Below is the cataloging for the media center's copies.

```
    Spelling program [machine-readable data file]. --
      [Uptown, Ill. : Northland Junior High School],
      1984.
      1 program file on 1 computer disk ; 5 1/4 in. + 1
   guide (1 p. ; 28 cm.)
      Title on label: Spelling for first graders.      Note 4
      Written by Ms. Smith's 6th grade class.          Note 6
      For first grade.                                 Note 14
      System requirements: Apple IIe; DOS 3.3.         Note 15
      Summary: Designed to teach beginning spelling.   Note 17
      1. Spelling--Study and teaching (Primary)--Com-
   puter programs. I. Apple IIe--DOS 3.3. II. Northland
   Junior High School (Uptown, Ill.). III. Title:
   Spelling for first graders.
```

Title/statement of responsibility: In this hypothetical program, the title was given in a title screen. The *Guidelines for Using AACR2 Chapter 9* say [Rule 9.0A]: "Non-commercially produced data files and program files for microcomputers (including locally produced microcomputer software) are not covered by the guidelines; catalog them according to the rules in Chapter 9." According to these rules, 9.0B1 and 9.0B2, and LCRI 1.4D1, the source for this title was from the prescribed source, and so was not enclosed in square brackets. Had it not been given on the title screen, then the accompanying documentation would be searched, and the *Visicalc* example would be followed, including Note 3, to indicate the source of the title.

Place, Publisher, date: LCRI 1.4D1 is followed here. The source is not written anywhere, but is known by the cataloger. Since the information did not come from a "prescribed source" listed in 9.0B2, but was known, it was added in brackets. The school was listed as the publisher, since it is the body with a continuing identity, and this information was placed in brackets because it was not given on the title screen or on accompanying material. The place given is the location of the school. The address was not given, although there was no ISBN given, since the software was cataloged for the media center at that school. If this "locally produced" software were cataloged for another library, the address could be given. The program was not copyrighted, so the "c" was not given before the date.

Notes: Note 4 gives a variation in the title, since the title on the label was different from the title on the title screen, a rather common occurrence. A note is imperative if the title on the label is placed in the tracings. Note 6 gives information about who produced this program. Note 10 describes the equipment and software needed to run the program. Note 14 gives the age level and came from the label. This note can be used "only when the information can be quoted from the publication." LCRI 2.7B14. In this instance, the grade level is indicated in the alternative title, given in Note 4. But teachers prefer the age level to be presented in a separate note, so it was given in the grade level note area. Note 17 was obtained from the students who wrote the program!

Tracings: The name of the "publisher" was traced, that is, the school. The computer system is given if the material is cataloged for one system.

Educational Software—
College Level

CHEM LAB SIM #3   V3.0   SER# 17094
COPYRIGHT(C)1979 BY HIGH TECHNOLOGY
SOFTWARE PRODUCTS, INC. /OKLA. STATE UNIV.

High Technology Software Products, Inc.
Oklahoma City, OK / All rights reserved worldwide

Label

```
---------------17094---------------
CHEM LAB SIMULATIONS      #3
1 -- CALORIMETRY
2 -- EXIT
          ENTER YOUR CHOICE _____
```

Screen 1

```
DEVELOPED BY DR. J. I. GELDER
COPYRIGHT (C) 1981 BY
OKLAHOMA STATE UNIVERSITY AND
HIGH TECHNOLOGY SOFTWARE PRODUCTS, INC.
```

Screen 2

Gelder, John I.
  Chem lab simulations. #3 [machine-readable data
file] : calorimetry / developed by J.I. Gelder. --
Version 3.0. -- Oklahoma City, Okla.
(P.O. Box 14665, Okla. City, OK 73113) : High
Technology Software Products, c1981.
  1 program file on 1 computer disk : col. ; 5 1/4
in. in manual, 31 cm. + 1 user's manual (20 p. ;
31 cm.).
  User's manual by John I. Gelder ; editor, Stan   Note 6
Funk (20 p. ; 31 cm.).
    System requirements: Apple II; Applesoft; 48K.   Note 15
    Summary: Simulates introductory college level   Note 17
chemistry experiments. Demonstrates Hess's Law by
having the user determine the heats of reaction of
three separate chemical reactions.
                          (Continued on next card)

Gelder, John I.
  Chem lab simulations. #3 [machine-readable data
file]...c1981. (Card 2).
  Contents: Heat capacity of the calorimeter -- Heat
of neutralization of HCl_{aq} and $NaOH_{aq}$ -- Heat of
solution of $NaOH_s$ -- Heat of reaction of HCl_{aq} and
$NaOH_s$ -- Hess' Law.
  High Technology: 17094.
  1. Calorimeters and calorimetry--Study and teach-
ing (Higher)--Computer programs. 2. Calorimeters and
calorimetry--Laboratory experiments. 3. Chemistry--
Apparatus--Computer programs. 4. Chemistry, Analytic
--Study and teaching (Higher)--Computer programs. I.
High Technology Software Products. II. Apple II--
Applesoft. III. Title. IV. Title: Calorimetry.

Title/Statement of responsibility: This was taken from the title screen, and was the same title as on the User's manual and on the disk label.

Place, Publisher, date: There was no ISBN given, so the address of the publisher was included.

Physical description: The disk is located in the 3-ring "User's manual." Since the name of the program on the screen and the manual were the same, the accompanying material information was given in this area. The manual was written by Dr. Gelder and edited by Stan Funk, and this added information about the authors of the manual is given in a note.

Notes: This needed both a contents note and a summary, which is rather unusual. It is more common to have either a contents note or a summary note.

Tracings: The make or model of the computer system is given. The programming language is given next, followed by the operating system, if known.

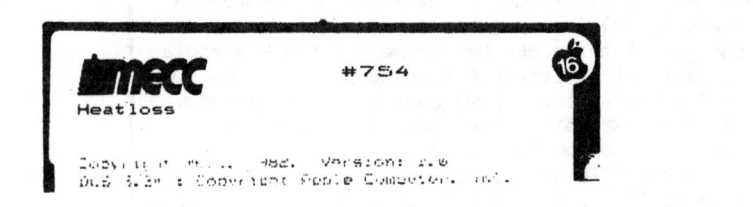

mecc   #754

Heatloss   Label

Copyright ... 48d. Version: 2.0
Dis 6.2" : Copyright Apple Computer, Inc.

MINNESOTA	HEATLOSSS	
EDUCATIONAL		
COMPUTING	VERSION 1.0	Screen 1
CONSORTIUM		
COPYRIGHT 1982		

```
    HEATLOSS
MINNESOTA STATE DEPARTMENT OF EDUCATION
DEPARTMENT OF ENERGY, PLANNING AND DEVELOPMENT          Screen 2
MINNESOTA EDUCATIONAL COMPUTING CONSORTIUM
```

```
          HEATLOSS
PROGRAM:
   1.  Heatloss
OTHER OPTIONS:                                          Screen 3
   2.  Program description
   3.  End
Which number?  _____
```

Heatloss [machine-readable data file] / Minnesota
   State Department of Education [and] Department of
   Energy, Planning and Development [and] Minnesota
   Educational Computing Consortium. -- Version 1.0.
   -- St. Paul, Minn. (3490 Lexington Avenue North,
   St. Paul, MN 55112) : Minnesota Educational
   Computing Consortium, c1982.
   1 program file on 1 computer disk ; 5 1/4 in. in
notebook, 31 cm. + 1 manual (60 p. : ill. ; 29 cm.).
   Coordinator, Karen Jostad ; developer, Doris Bower   Note 6
; programmer, Rick Anderson.
   Based on earlier module by: Dick Clark, Neal   Note 7
Prachnow.
   For grades 7-adult.   Note 14
   System requirements: Apple II; DOS 3.3.   Note 15
   Summary: Calculates the heat lost through various   Note 17
parts of the house and the possible dollar savings
with rennovation.
                          (Continued on next card)

```
Heatloss [machine-readable data file] ... c1982.
  (Card 2).
Formulas/data from: ASHRAE handbook, 1981 funda-      Note 18
mentals. New York : American Society of Heating, Re-
frigerating and Air-Conditioning Engineers, Inc. --
Home energy disclosure manual / Rick Anderson, et
al. St. Paul, Minn. : Minnesota Energy Agency, 1981.
  MECC: #754.                                           Note 19
  1. Insulation, (Heat)--Analysis--Study and teach-
ing (Higher)--Computer programs. 2. Dwellings--
Insulation--Analysis--Computer programs. I. Minne-
sota State Department of Education. II. Minnesota
Department of Energy, Planning and Development. III.
Minnesota Educational Computing Consortium. IV.
Apple II--DOS 3.3.
```

Place, Publisher, date: The address was listed because the ISBN number was not given.

Physical description: The name of the manual is the same as the name of the program on the title screen, so the manual may be included as accompanying material in the physical description area.

Notes: Notes 6-7 came from p. 56 of the manual. Another note 7 was taken from the label. Note 14 was taken from from p. 2 of the manual. Note 17 was taken from an introductory screen. Note 18 was taken from p. 51 of the manual. The punctuation followed the instructions given in 1.7A3 where the punctuation used in the main body is followed in the notes, except whenever the prescribed punctuation should be a space, dash, dash, space, it will be substituted in the notes by a single space. Note 19 came from the label.

PUBLIC DOMAIN SOFTWARE

This disk is part of Commodore's public domain software. After the cataloger brings up the menu or directory screen, the individual program's screens should be examined. Looking at the individual title screens prevents listing a name in the contents as a title of a program when it is not a program.

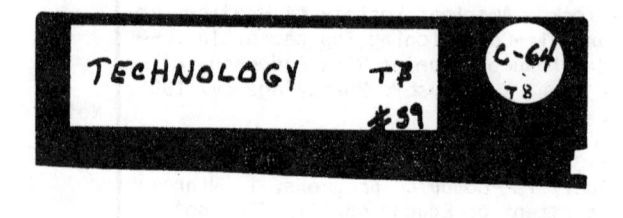

Label

```
  0    "TECHNOLOGY       "  TB  2A
  4       "CBM 4032 V.2.1"    PRG
 38       "RESIST TEST V.C2"  PRG
 86       "RESISTORS.C2"      PRG
 48       "SIMULATION.C2"     PRG
488   BLOCKS FREE.
```

Screen 1
a "Menu"

This is not a title screen, but a "menu" (sometimes called directory or catalog) screen. Each of the names listed were searched, and there was no program called Technology or "CBM 4032" on the disk. As the copies of the title screens below show, there are only three programs on this disk.

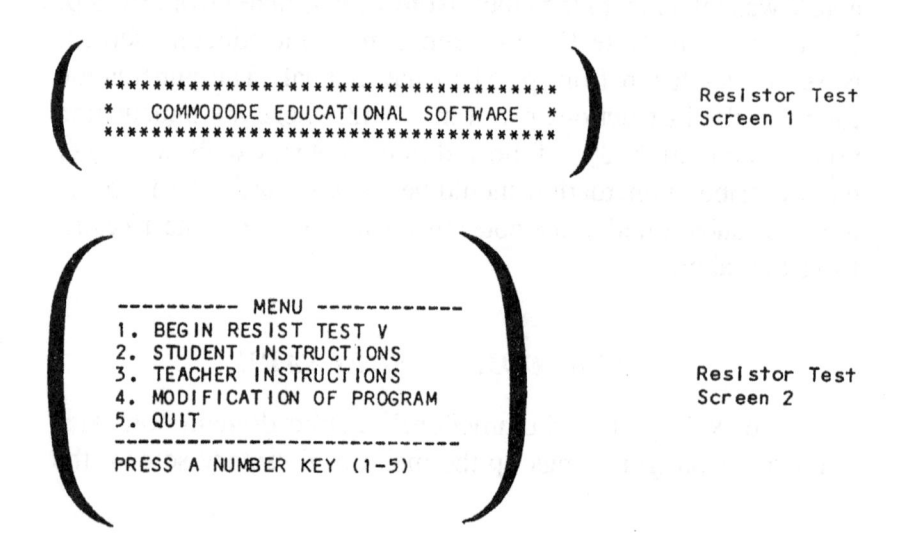

```
***************************************
*   COMMODORE EDUCATIONAL SOFTWARE   *
***************************************
```

Resistor Test
Screen 1

```
---------- MENU ------------
1. BEGIN RESIST TEST V
2. STUDENT INSTRUCTIONS
3. TEACHER INSTRUCTIONS
4. MODIFICATION OF PROGRAM
5. QUIT
----------------------------
PRESS A NUMBER KEY (1-5)
```

Resistor Test
Screen 2

Resistor Test
#2 Screen 1

This is a test on visualizing resistance
circuits and calculating the total value of
resistance in a variety of possible circuits.
When you are running the test, you are being
timed. Whenever you run this test, try and
see if you can beat your old times. Run the
program for further instructions.
    press space bar to continue

Resistor Test
#3 Screen 1

```
RESISTOR TEST                    TEACHER INST. 1
------------------------------------------------
TO THE BEST OF OUR KNOWLEDGE, THIS PROGRAM
IS IN THE PUBLIC DOMAIN.  IF THIS IS NOT THE
CASE PLEASE CONTACT:
            3370 PHARMACY AVE.
            AGINCOURT, ONTARIO
            CANADA M1W 2K4
            (416) 499-4292
```

Resistor Test
#3 Screen 2

```
RESISTOR TEST                    TEACHER INST. 2
------------------------------------------------
    Program name: Resistor Test V
    Written by:   Unknown
    Upgraded by:
    This program will run on any
    BASIC 2.0  PET COMPUTER
    BASIC 4.0  PET COMPUTER
    8032  CBM  COMPUTER
    COMMODORE 64 COMPUTER
    Press space bar to continue
```

```
****************************************
*   COMMODORE EDUCATIONAL SOFTWARE   *
****************************************
```

Resistors
Screen 1

```
---------- MENU ------------
1. BEGIN RESISTOR LESSON
2. STUDENT INSTRUCTIONS
3. TEACHER INSTRUCTIONS
4. QUIT
----------------------------
PRESS A NUMBER KEY (1-4)
```

Resistors
Screen 2

```
Resistors (Continued)
    Program name: Resistors
    Written by: R.W. Dray
    Upgraded by: Arman Aiello
    This program will run on any
    BASIC 2.0   PET COMPUTER
    BASIC 4.0 PET COMPUTER
    8032  CBM   COMPUTER
            only
    Press space bar to continue
```

Resistors #2
Screen 1

Resistors #2
Screen 2

```
This program reviews resistors both in parallel
and series circuits.  At the end of the review
the student is given the option of doing some
questions.  A pencil, paper and a calculator
would be beneficial to the student.
```

Resistors #3
Screen 1

```
RESISTORS                    TEACHER INST. 1
--------------------------------------------
TO THE BEST OF OUR KNOWLEDGE, THIS PROGRAM
IS IN THE PUBLIC DOMAIN.  IF THIS IS NOT THE
CASE PLEASE CONTACT:
            3370 PHARMACY AVE.
            AGINCOURT, ONTARIO
            CANADA M1W 2K4
            (416) 499-4292
```

```
( ********************************************* )
  *   COMMODORE EDUCATIONAL SOFTWARE   *
  *********************************************
```
Simulation
Screen 1

```
(  ----------- MENU ------------- )
   1. BEGIN SIMULATION
   2. STUDENT INSTRUCTIONS
   3. TEACHER INSTRUCTIONS
   4. QUIT
   -------------------------------
   PRESS A NUMBER KEY (1-4)
```
Resistor Test
Screen 2

```
( Simulation:                                    )
  How the computer follows a simple program.
  The program that you will see will add two
  numbers and print the result.
```
Simulation
#2 Screen 1

```
( <A simple flow chart> )
```
Simulation
#2 Screen 2

```
( SIMULATION                    TEACHER INST. 1 )
  -------------------------------------------------
  TO THE BEST OF OUR KNOWLEDGE, THIS PROGRAM
  IS IN THE PUBLIC DOMAIN.  IF THIS IS NOT THE
  CASE PLEASE CONTACT:
           3370 PHARMACY AVE.
           AGINCOURT, ONTARIO
           CANADA M1W 2K4
           (416) 499-4292
```
Simulation
#3 Screen 1

```
SIMULATION                          TEACHER INST. 2      Simulation
-------------------------------------------------          #3 Screen 2
    Program name: Simulation
    Written by:    Unknown
    Upgraded by:
    This program will run on any
    BASIC 2.0  PET COMPUTER
    BASIC 4.0 PET COMPUTER
    8032  CBM  COMPUTER
    COMMODORE 64 COMPUTER
    Press space bar to continue
```

The following is the correct way to catalog this disk, since the menu listed a collective title.

```
Technology [machine-readable data file]. --
    Agincourt, Canada (3370 Pharmacy Ave., Agincourt,
    Ontario, Canada M1W 2K4) : Commodore Educational
    Software, [1981?].
    3 program files on 1 computer disk ; 5 1/4 in.
    Programs are in the public domain.              Note 9
    System requirements: Commodore 64.              Note 15
    Programs: Resist test V: Timed test on visualizing   Note 17
resistance circuits and calculating the total value
of resistance in a variety of circuits -- Resistors:
Reviews parallel and series circuits -- Simulation:
How the computer follows a simple program; and how
to read a flow chart.
    1. Electric resistors--Study and teaching (Higher)
--Computer programs. 2. Electronics--Study and
teaching (Higher)--Computer programs. 3. Programming
(Electronic computers)--Study and teaching. I.
Commodore 64. II. Title: Resist test V. III. Title:
Resistors. IV. Title: Simulation.
```

Title/statement of responsibility: ''Technology'' is taken to be the collective title for the disk, and comes from the main ''menu.'' The last three names on the ''menu'' are the titles of individual programs on the disk.

Place, Publisher, date: The publisher and place were given on the title screens of the three programs, and the date was estimated.

Physical description: The menu listed the programs, and each title was searched, thus the cataloger knows there are three files on this disk, and includes this information.

Notes: Note 9 tells the patron that this material is in the public domain, hence it may be freely copied. Note 17 is a contents note that begins with the word "Programs," instead of "Contents." The punctuation for Note 17 tries to make it clear to the patron what information belongs with each title.

Tracings: The first added entry is for the computer system. The three added title tracings are for the three separate programs on this disk. The collective title of the disk is "Technology."

Exploring how the publisher produced this disk might help to explain the grouping of these dissimilar programs onto one disk. These separate programs were owned by one publisher, or else are in "the public domain," meaning they are not copyrighted. When the publisher wanted to produce a "new" title, he used programs he thought would sell as a package, and put them on a disk. It is possible these programs have been published before on another disk. Gathering independent items and reissuing them under a new title is not new in nonbook publishing. It is done with sound recordings, video recordings, slides, pictures, and kits, to name the most prevalent examples. The catalog needs to include the titles of the individual parts, so the order clerk can see that the library owns these individual parts, and not order what will later prove to be duplicate programs. For this reason, as well as for the needs of patrons, the cataloger traces the titles of the individual programs. Listing individual titles is common practice when cataloging nonbook material.

EXAMPLE FOR NONCOLLECTIVE TITLE CATALOGING

The disk above will be cataloged now in a different manner, in order to show how to catalog a disk lacking a collective title, according to AACR2 1.1G. The example given above for this disk is the correct one, while the second example is contrived to illustrate cataloging a noncollective title entry, and is not intended to show the correct way to catalog this disk. Most people who do not catalog daily find remembering the method and punctuation for cataloging noncollective titles a bit of a chore because the procedures are slightly different. The noncollective title option in AACR2 is a necessary "last resort," and catalogers should know how to use it when necessary.

LCRI 1.1G2 states: "If, in an item lacking a collective title, no one part predominates, either describe the item as a unit . . ." as shown below, or by using 'with' notes. "If describing the item as a unit, record the titles of the individually titled parts in the order in which they are named in the chief source of information or in the order in which they appear in the item if there is no single chief source of information. Separate the titles of the parts by semicolons if the parts are all by the same person . . ." Parts not from the same person or body are separated by a period between each title.

The previous disk is cataloged below *as if* there were no collective title, called "Technology":

```
   4       "CBM 4032 V.2.1"    PRG
  38       "RESIST TEST V.C2"  PRG        Screen 1
  86       "RESISTORS.C2"      PRG        a "menu"
  48       "SIMULATION.C2"     PRG
 488   BLOCKS FREE.
```

and the title screens for the individual programs remain the same as given for Technology.

This is hypothetical, just an illustration for noncollective titles.

```
Resist test V. Resistors / R.W. Dray, Arman Aiello.
  Simulation [machine-readable data file]. --
Agincourt, Ontario (3370 Pharmacy Ave., Agincourt,
Ontario, Canada M1W 2K4) : Commodore Educational
Software, [1981?].
3 program files on 1 computer disk ; 5 1/4 in.
Public domain software.                               Note 9
System requirements: Commodore 64.                    Note 15
  Programs: Resist test V: Timed test on visualizing  Note 17
resistance circuits and calculating the total value
of resistance in a variety of circuits -- Resistors:
Reviews parallel and series circuits -- Simulation:
How the computer follows a simple program; and how
to read a flow chart.
  1. Electric resistors--Study and teaching (Higher)
--Computer programs. 2. Electronics--Study and
teaching (Higher)--Computer programs. 3. Programming
(Electronic computers)--Study and teaching. I. Dray,
R.W. II. Aiello, Arman. III. Commodore 64. IV.
Title: Resistors. V. Title: Simulation.
```

Had the parts all been by the same person, the separation between each title would have been a semicolon, and the catalog
record would look like:

```
KnowWho, You.
  Resist test V ; Resistors ; Simulation [machine-
readable data file] / by You KnowWho. -- Agincourt,
```

Label

```
        RANDOM HOUSE
         MICRO-LINE
          PROGRAMS
PRESS RETURN TO GO TO NEXT MENU
```

Screen 1

```
        READABILITY ANALYSIS
        A MICRO LINE PROGRAM
COPYRIGHT (C) 1980, BY RANDOM HOUSE, INC.
    PRESS <RETURN> TO CONTINUE? ____
```

Screen 2

```
        THIS IS YOUR
READABILITY ANALYSIS PROGRAM
  PRESS <RETURN> TO CONTINUE? ____
```

Screen 3

```
    Readability analysis [machine-readable data file].
      -- [New York, N.Y.] : Random House, c1980.
      1 program file on 1 computer disk ; 5 1/4 in. in
    notebook + 1 guide (10, 13, [25] p. ; 31 cm.). --
    (Micro line program).
        System requirements: Apple II; 48K; DOS 3.3.        Note 15
      Summary: This program enables one to estimate the    Note 17
    grade level of trade books, reference books, and
    letters, ranging from first grade through college
    level.
        Indexes used: Grades 1-3. Wheeler/Smith Index.      Note 18
    Spache Index. Dale-Chall Word List -- Grades 4-
    Adult. Dale-Chall Index. Fog Index. Flesch Grade
    Level. Smog Index.
      ISBN 0-394-90321-6.                                    ISBN
                           (Continued on next card)
```

```
    Readability analysis [machine-readable data file]
      ... c1980. (Card 2).
      1. Reading--Analysis--Computer programs. I. Random
    House. II. Apple II--DOS 3.3. III. Wheeler/Smith In-
    dex. IV. Spache Index. V. Dale-Chall Word List. VI.
    Dale-Chall Index. VII. Fog Index. VIII. Flesch Grade
    Level. IX. Smog Index. X. Series.
```

Title: The title is from the title screens.

Physical description: The disk is located in the notebook. The title page of the accompanying material reads: *Readability Analysis Program (RAP),* and the cataloger considered this similar to the title screen, not a distinct title.

Notes: The information about the system requirements is on the label. Listing the contents of the sections follows the pattern given in AACR2 1.7B18 nd 5.7B18. The ISBN number is given on the label.

Educational Game Software

Label

```
        SPINNAKER SOFTWARE PRESENTS...
STORY
      MACHINE
COPYRIGHT (C) 1982, 1983
     SPINNAKER SOFTWARE CORP.
     ALL RIGHTS RESERVED
```

Screen 1

```
     PRESS 1-5 TO PLAY
1)  WATCH A STORY.
2)  TAKE TURNS WRITING A STORY.
3)  WRITE YOUR OWN STORY.
4)  WATCH A STORY YOU'VE SAVED BEFORE.
5)  MAKE UP NAMES FOR CHARACTERS.
```

Screen 2

51

```
Spinnaker Software presents... story machine
 [machine-readable data file]. -- Cambridge,
 MA (215 First St., Cambridge, MA 02142)
  : Spinnaker Software, c1983.
  1 program file on 1 computer cartridge : sd.,
 col. ; 3 in. in box, 23 x 17 x 3 cm. + 1 booklet
 (10 p. ; 13 cm.). -- (Early learning series).
  Creator, DesignWare.
  System requirements: Commodore 64.        Note 6
  For ages 5-9.                             Note 15
  Summary: Educational game to assist writing   Note 14
sentences, paragraphs and simple stories. The sen-  Note 17
tences will be acted out on the screen.
  1. English language--Composition and exercise--
Study and teaching (Primary)--Computer programs. 2.
English language--Paragraphs--Study and teaching
(Primary)--Computer programs. 3. English language--
Rhetoric--Sentences--Study and teaching (Primary)--
Computer programs. I. Spinnaker (Firm). II.
DesignWare (Firm). III. Commodore 64. IV. Title:
Story machine. V. Series.
```

Title/statement of responsibility: The title came from the title screen.

Place, Publisher, date: The address was given because there was no ISBN given. The copyright date was taken from the title screens.

Physical description: The title of the booklet is: *Story Machine.* On the back of the booklet it says: "Package and Instruction Booklet Illustration: Bill Morrison." To be included in a catalog record, the author or illustrator needs to be listed on the title page, outside of the package, or other noticeable place. By listing the name on the back of the booklet, Spinnaker is indicating Mr. Morrison made only a limited contribution to this package, and the cataloger will not include Mr. Morrison on the catalog record.

Notes: Note 6 is added because the back of the box and the back cover of the instruction booklet say: "DesignWare, creators of *Story Machine* is a company of educators and computer professionals specializing in computer programs for children.'' The cataloger considered this company important, included the note and traced the company. Note 14 gives the age level and came from cover of the box. This note is used ''only when the information can be quoted from the publication.'' LCRI 2.7B14. Note 17 was adapted from information on the cover.

Tracings: The firm in the publisher field was traced. The computer system is given when the material is for one system. Most series titles are traced in microcomputer software, as it provides yet another access point for both patrons and librarians.

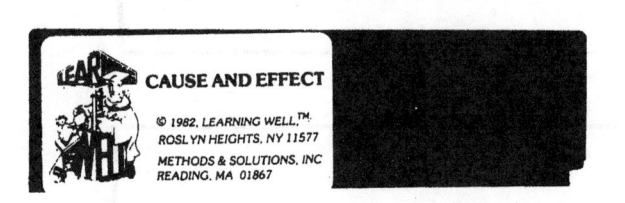

CAUSE AND EFFECT

© 1982, LEARNING WELL,™.
ROSLYN HEIGHTS, NY 11577

METHODS & SOLUTIONS, INC
READING, MA 01867

Label

```
          CAUSE
           AND
          EFFECT
    BLUE LEVEL EDITION
        CREATED BY
       LEARNING WELL
 200 SOUTH SERVICE ROAD
  ROSLYN HEIGHTS, N.Y.
    MICRO ADAPTATION
  METHODS AND SOLUTIONS
       READING, MA
       VERSION 1.1
  PRESS ANY KEY TO CONTINUE
```

Screen 1

```
DO YOU WANT INSTRUCTIONS (Y OR N)
```

Screen 2

```
  Cause and effect [machine-readable data file] /
    created by Learning Well. -- Blue level ed., Ver-
    sion 1.1. -- Roslyn Heights, N.Y. (200 S. Service
    Rd., Roslyn Heights, NY 11577) : Learning Well,
    c1982.                                                  Note 4
    1 program file on 1 computer disk : col. ; 5 1/4
  in. In box, 23 x 16 x 2 cm. + 1 guide ([7] p. ;          Note 6
  22 cm.).
    Title on box: Professor Davensteev's Cause and         Note 14
  effect.                                                   Note 15
    Developer, David Savitsky ; computer adaptor,
  Methods & Solutions, Inc.
    For grades 3-5.
    System requirements: Apple II; 48K.
                              (Continued on next card)
```

```
  Cause and effect [machine-readable data file] ...
    c1982. (Card 2).
    Summary: Game for 2-6 players. Object is to be
  first to reach top of mountain. Player will read a       Note 17
  paragraph and determine either the cause or effect.
    Learning Well: AC 601.                                 Note 19
    1. Causation--Study and teaching (Elementary)--
  Computer programs. I. Savitsky, David. II. Learning
  Well (Firm). III. Apple II. IV. Title: Professor
  Davensteev's Cause and effect.
```

The following "see" references lead the patron from the subjects "Cause" and "Effect" to the single subject heading used in the *Library of Congress Subject Headings,* 9th edition.

```
Cause and effect
                See
Causation
```

```
Effect and cause
                See
Causation
```

Statement of responsibility: This appeared 'prominently' on the title screen.

Edition/Version: This came from the title screen. AACR2 states in 1.2B3: "In case of doubt whether a statement is an edition statement, take the presence of such words as *edition, issue, version* (or their equivalents in other languages) as evidence that such a statement is an edition statement, and record it as such." See AACR2 1.2D1, 1.2E1, and 2.2D1 for examples of the punctuation when two "editions" are listed.

Place, Publisher, date: The address was given because there was no ISBN given. The copyright date was taken from the title screen.

Physical description: The cover of the booklet states:

CAUSE AND EFFECT
By Learning Well™
BLUE LEVEL EDITION
Computer Adaption—Methods & Solutions, Inc.

and this is clearly the same title, edition, and even author as the title screen, so the information about accompanying material is placed as accompanying material. The pages of the guide are not numbered, so the cataloger counted the pages and placed the number in brackets, according to AACR2, 2.5B3: "When recording the number of unnumbered pages, etc., either give the estimated number preceded by *ca.*, without square brackets, or enclose the exact number in square brackets."

Notes: Note 6 came from [p. 1] of guide. Note 14 gives the age level and came from both the cover of the box and [p. 1] of the guide. This note is used "only when the information can be quoted from the publication." LCRI 2.7B14. Note 17 was adapted from [p. 1] of the guide. Note 19 came from the cover of the box.

Tracings: "Learning Well" was both creator and publisher and was traced. The computer system was given.

Label

```
/                                                    \
(           Crossword Magic                          )          Screen 1
(             Maker Disk                              )
(                by                                   )
(           Larry Sherman                            )
( copyright (C) 1981 L&S Computerware                )
( P.O. Box 70728  Sunnyvale, CA 94086                )
\                                                    /
```

```
/                                                    \
(          Crossword Magic 3.0                        )
(             by Larry Sherman                        )
( (1) Create a puzzle                                 )
( (2) Print a puzzle                                  )
( (3) Transfer puzzle                                 )          Screen 2
( (4) Delete a picture                                )
( (5) Complete puzzle                                 )
( (6) Edit a puzzle                                   )
( (7) Exit program                                    )
( Select (1-7)                                        )
\                                                    /
```

```
+------------------------------------------------------+
|                                                      |
|   Sherman, Larry.                                    |
|     Crossword magic [machine-readable data file] /   |
|   by Larry Sherman. -- Version 3.0. -- Sunnyvale, CA |
|   (P.O. Box 70728, Sunnyvale, CA 94086) : L&S        |
|   Computerware, c1981.                               |     Note 15
|     1 program file on 1 computer disk : double sides,|     Note 17
|   col. ; 5 1/4 in. in container, 13 x 16 x 1 cm. +   |
|   1 guide ([4] p. ; 22 cm.).                         |     Note 18
|     System requirements: Apple II+; 48K; DOS 3.3.    |
|     Summary: For constructing British non-symetrical |
|   puzzles.                                           |
|     Contains: Maker disk -- Demonstration disk.      |
|     1. Crossword puzzles--Computer programs. I. L & S|
|   Computerware. II. Apple II--DOS 3.3. III. Title.   |
|                                                      |
+------------------------------------------------------+
```

Title/statement of responsibility: Taken from the title screen. Do not confuse ownership of the copyright with the name of the author.

Place, Publisher, date: The address was given because there was no ISBN given. The copyright date was taken from the title screen.

Physical description: "double sides" follows the form given in 8.5C6. If there were color and sound included, this part of the physical description would look like:

: double sides, sd., col.

The guide is really just instructions, without its own name, issued at the same time as the program, and an integral part of the whole package, and so is included as accompanying material.

Notes: The system requirements were taken from the guide, page 3. The summary was adapted from the verso of the guide's cover.

Business-Oriented Software

A spreadsheet, a filing or mailing list program, and a word-processing program will be cataloged, illustrating how easily the different types of programs can be cataloged by the MRDF rules.

Label

Screen 1

[Visicalc] [machine-readable data file] / Software
  Arts. -- San Jose, CA (2895 Zanker Rd, San Jose,
  CA 95134) : VisiCorp, c1981.
  1 program file on 1 computer disk ; 5 1/4 in. in
box, 27 x 20 x 5 cm.
  Title from the label.   Note 3
  System requirements: Apple II or higher; 48K.   Note 10
  User's guide by Dan Fylstra and Bill Kling (ca.   Note 11
200 p. : ill. ; 24 cm.).
  Summary: Electronic worksheet to calculate and   Note 17
display numbers in budgets, charts, statistics,
graphs, etc.
  1. Accounting--Computer programs. 2. Machine
accounting--Computer programs. I. Visicorp (Firm).
II. Apple II.

59

Title/statement of authority: The "chief source of information" for the title is the title screen. The title screen for this program does not include the title of the program, but actually gives a blank spreadsheet form, and copyright information. Thus the title was taken from the label, which is listed in *Guidelines for Using AACR2 Chapter 9 for Cataloging Microcomputer Software* as the second acceptable source for the title. AACR2 says in 1.1A2: "Take information recorded in this area [title/statement of responsibility] from the chief source of information for the material to which the item being described belongs. Enclose information supplied from any other source in square brackets." Since the title did not come from the chief source, the title is enclosed in square brackets, and a Note 3 is added to tell where the title came from.

Place, Publisher, date: The address was given because there was no ISBN given. The copyright date was taken from the screen.

Physical description: The manual is not listed in accompanying material because the title page of the manual lists its authors as separate and distinct from the company who authored the program.

Notes: Note 3 gives the source of the title which is given in square brackets. Note 11 describes the manual, and follows the form given in AACR2 2.7B11. Note 15 describes the equipment and software needed to run the program, and the cataloger does not know whether this program will run on an Apple IIe or Apple IIc, so the two systems listed on the title page of the manual, the outside of the box, and on the label of the disk were mentioned.

Tracings: The firm in the publisher field was traced. The computer systems are given.

Label

```
PFS: FILE FUNCTION MENU
1   DESIGN FILE    4   SEARCH/UPDATE
2   ADD            5   PRINT
3   COPY           6   REMOVE
        SELECTION NUMBER:
        FILE NAME:
(C) 1983   Software Publishing Corp.

After hitting Control C>
```
Screen 1

After hitting Control C >

```
Design File Menu
1   Create file
2   Change design
        Selection number:
```
Screen 2

```
        Put diskette in Drive 1
                Warning
    The diskette in Drive 1 will
        be completely over-written
Press ESC to abandon this operation
    Press Control-C to continue
```
Screen 3

```
PFS file [machine-readable data file]. -- Mountain
    View, CA (1901 Landings Drive, Mt. View, CA 94043)
    : Software Publishing Corp., c1983.
    1 program file on 1 computer disk ; 5 1/4 in. in
box, 24 x 18 x 2 cm. + 1 manual (ca. 200 p. ;
23 cm.).
    Program authors, John Page and D.D. Roberts.       Note 6
    Manual by Rose Mack (ca. 200 p. ; 23 cm.).         Note 11
    System requirements: Apple IIe; 64K; 80 columns;   Note 15
2 disk drives; printer.
    Summary: A personal filing system.                 Note 17
    1. Indexing--Computer programs. 2. Files and
filing (Documents)--Computer programs. I. Software
Publishing Corporation (Firm). II. Apple IIe. III.
Title: File..
```

Title/statement of responsibility: The title came from the title screen.

Place, Publisher, date: The address was given because there was no ISBN given. The address came from the back of the box. The copyright date was taken from the title screen.

Physical description: The user's manual was divided into many sections, so the page numbers are approximated.

Notes: Note 6 came from the cover of the user's manual, and was included as additional identification of this program, since there are other programs in the PFS group, such as *PFS Report*, etc. All three names are in small type at the bottom of the manual's cover, and the cataloger did not consider the names worth tracing. Note 15 describes the equipment and software needed to run the program.

Tracings: The firm in the publisher field was traced. The computer system is given when the cataloged material is for one system.

Label

```
       The Bank Street Writer
            Developed by
      Intentional Educations, Inc.
        Franklin E. Smith and
  (C) 1983   The Bank Street College
           of Education
      Programmer: Gene Kusmiak
Commodore version: Charles Olson, Jr.
Please wait a moment while the program
Is loading.
           Scholastic Inc.
```

Screen 1

```
Bank Street writer [machine-readable data file] /
    developed by Intentional Educations, Inc., Frank-
    lin E. Smith and The Bank Street College of Educ-
    ation. -- Commodore version / Charles Olson, Jr.
    -- New York, N.Y. : Scholastic, c1983.
    1 program file on 3 identical computer disks ;
5 1/4 in. In book, 29 cm. + 1 handbook (ca. 50 p. ;
29 cm. + 1 manual (35 p. ; 15 cm.).
    Disks in notebook.                              Note 10
    System requirementes: Commodore 64.             Note 15
    Summary: Word processing program.               Note 17
    ISBN 0-590-92739-6.                             ISBN
    1. Word processing (Office practice). I. Smith,
Franklin E. II. Scholastic (Firm). III. Bank Street
College of Education. IV. Intentional Educations
(Firm). V. Commodore 64.
```

Place, Publisher, date: The address was not given because there was an ISBN number.

Physical description: The two guides were very different in size and pagination.

Some libraries, using this basic catalog record for their cataloging, will permit only one disk to circulate and will remove information about the other disks on the catalog record.

Simplification Methods for MRDF Cataloging

These examples were presented to help solve many of the cataloging problems with machine-readable data files, as of 1985. New opportunities in cataloging are constantly presented by publishers, distributors and authors. There is no time to sit back and look around for new worlds to conquer. Guidelines, rules, and manuals make the cataloger's work easier, but cataloging machine-readable data files still requires considerable time and effort. Two short cuts are shown below. One is a partially filled in catalog card (or an OCLC work form, which is not a part of this work) to help with spacing, punctuation, and remembering some common points. Here is one:

```
        .
        .                    [machine-readable data file]
    /                        -- Version      . --                  :
                     , c198 .
        1 program file (              ) on 1 computer disk :
    col. ; 5 1/4 in. in box, 17 x 3 x 10 cm. + 1
    guide ( ˚ p. ;      cm.). -- (                  ).
        Producer, Jojo Smith ; programmer,                  Note 6
        For grades                                          Note 14
        System requirements: IBM-PC; 128K;            .     Note 15
        Summary:                                            Note 17


                         (Continued on next card)
```

```
       .
       .                    [machine-readable data file]
    ... c198 . (Card 2).

       Contents:                        --           --   Note 18

                                                            Note 19

       ISBN                                                 ISBN
       1.                                  2.
    Computer programs. 3.              --Computer programs

       I.               (Firm). II. IBM-PC. III. Title. IV.
    Title:
```

Tracing could be: Apple II—Applesoft BASIC—DOS 3.3. Note 19 is publisher's number.

For a library needing only the briefest cataloging, the following suggestions provide for this while maintaining bibliographic integrity which will permit later transfer of most of these brief records to an online catalog by making "hits" against a large cataloging database. The following is the "basic" information needed:

1. Title proper (this is the complete information before [machine-readable data file]). This should be complete and taken from the title screen. If it is from the label, it should be bracketed. Hopefully, it will include a Note 3 saying the title is from the label.
2. Version, if available.
3. Publisher.
4. Year.

There may be discrepancies between the date on the screen, the date on the printed material, and the date on the label. Take the date from the screen as authentic for the material being cataloged. The other dates may be for other versions, the copyright for the printed material, etc.

5. Extant.
   What kind of machine does this require?
   How many computer disks or cartridges are in the set?
6. Author, if available.
7. ISBN, if available.
   If the ISBN is available, it can be used to locate this specific item on a national database. See references to ISBN in AACR2 1.8E1, and in Appendix D, under Standard number.

Using these items, plus the notes for system requirements and variant titles, as the "basics" for a catalog entry, the computer software cataloged in the first section of this work will be shown again, this time with "simplified" cataloging. The subject headings remain the same as before.

```
Koetke, Walter.
   Survival math [machine-readable data file]. --
Version 1.0. -- Sunburst Communications, c1983.
   1 program file on 1 computer disk : col. ; +
1 guide.
   System requirements: Commodore 64.          Note 15
   Sunburst: #1084.                             Note 19
   1. Arithmetic--Study and teaching (Secondary)--
Computer programs. 2. Business mathematics--Study
and teaching (Secondary)--Computer programs. 3. Con-
sumer education--Study and teaching (Secondary)--
Computer programs. I. Sunburst Communications
(Firm). II. Commodore 64. III. Title.
```

Vocabulary skills [machine-readable data file] :
prefixes, suffixes and root words. -- Milton
Bradley Co., c1983.
1 program file on 1 computer disk ; in box,
38 x 3 x 24 cm.
With Microcomputer software guide and a set of   Note 11
worksheets and quizzes.
System requirements: Apple II; 48K; DOS 3.3;   Note 15
Applesoft BASIC.
MB: 7882.   Note 19
1. Vocabulary--Study and teaching (Elemenatary)--
Computer programs. 2. Language arts--Computer
programs. 3. Word recognition--Study and teaching
(Elementary)--Computer programs. I. Milton Bradley
Company. II. Apple II--Applesoft BASIC--DOS 3.3.
III. Title: Prefixes, suffixes, and root words.

Commodore 64 Logo [machine-readable data file]. --
Commodore Business Machines, c1982.
1 program file on 2 computer disks : col.
With Commmodore 64 Logo tutorial.   Note 11
System requirements: Commodore 64.   Note 15
1. Logo (Computer program language). I. Commodore
Business Machines. II. Commodore 64. III. Title:
Logo.

Higgins, Douglas
Microcomputer workshops presents English
achievement [machine-readable data file]. -- Microcomputer Workshops Courseware, c1982.
5 program files on 5 computer disks + 5 manuals.
System requirements: Apple II; 48K; DOS 3.3.   Note 15
1. English Achievement Test--Study and teaching--
Computer programs. 2. English language--Grammar--
Study and teaching--Computer programs. I. Microcomputer Workshops Courseware (Firm). II. Apple II.
III. Title. IV. Title: English achievement.

Elementary. Volume 4 [machine-readable data file].
  Version 4.2. -- Sunburst Communications, c1980.
  1 program file on 1 computer disk : col. ; in
notebook, 29 cm.
  Title on disk and cover of guide: Ecology,   Note 11
astronomy and arithmetic.
  System requirements: Apple II; DOS 3.3.   Note 15
  Sunburst: #995.   Note 19
  MECC: TX 472-179.
  1. Ecology--Study and teaching (Elementary)--Com-
puter programs. 2. Astronomy--Study and teaching
(Elementary)--Computer programs. 3. Arithmetic--
Study and teaching (Elementary)--Computer programs.
I. Sunburst Communications (Firm). II. Apple II--DOS
3.3. III. Title: Ecology, astronomy and arithmetic.

Spelling program [machine-readable data file]. --
  [Northland Junior High School], 1984.
  1 program file on 1 computer disk + 1 guide
  Title on label: Spelling for first graders.   Note 4
  Written by Ms. Smith's 6th grade class.   Note 6
  System requirements: Apple IIe; DOS 3.3.   Note 15
  1. Spelling--Study and teaching (Primary)--Com-
puter programs. I. Apple IIe--DOS 3.3. II. Northland
Junior High School (Uptown, III.). III. Title:
Spelling for first graders.

The Future

Looking at the future we see the ISBN as a unique identification number which will help provide positive identification of software and is currently assigned by Bowker. When the number is on the software it should be included in the catalog record. There may be some error by publishers and catalogers in copying this number, but it is a useful identifier. For catalogers inputting machine-readable data file records into a national data base, following national guidelines is imperative, and the guidelines can be located in:

> *Anglo-American Cataloguing Rules.* 2nd ed. Chicago: American Library Association, 1978, supplemented by:
> *Guidelines for Using AACR2 Chapter 9 for Cataloging Microcomputer Software.* Chicago: American Library Association, 1984, supplemented by:
> *Cataloging Service Bulletin.* Washington, D.C.: Library of Congress, Processing Services, 1978-

Other useful materials are:

> *Machine-readable Data Files Format.* Dublin, Ohio: OCLC, 1984. This is the OCLC manual with instructions for working with this format on their data base.
> And the comparable manuals from RLIN, UTLAS, WLN, and other networks for cataloging this format.

Catalogers need to remain aware of existing, proposed and needed standards for microcomputer software by national associations, such as the American National Standards Institute, and National Information Standards Organization. The American

Library Association's Library and Information Technology Association, Technical Standards for Library Automation Committee (TESLA) also has an interest in these standards and attending these TESLA meetings at the ALA conferences, as well as reading about their activity in their publications: *Information Technology and Libraries,* and *LITA Newsletter* will help one stay reasonably current.

Other publications having articles on cataloging microcomputer software include: *Cataloging and Classification Quarterly, Technical Services Quarterly* from The Haworth Press, and *Library Resources and Technical Services,* another publication of the American Library Association.

Many libraries are providing microcomputer software for their patrons to use and to check out, so bibliographic control is a necessity. The proliferation of different operating systems is likely to continue for several years. Library patrons find paper copies of bibliographies very attractive and convenient. Librarians can "download" full online cataloging records to prepare these bibliographies. The short bibliography shown below was prepared by "downloading" the cataloging records shown earlier for Cause and effect, Crossword magic and Story machine, and then deleting information not necessary in the printed bibliography. The title proper, that information before [machine-readable data file], was kept intact, as was the statement of responsibility. The version was kept, and place, publisher, and date.

The physical description was abbreviated to contain only the most basic information. Then the entries were rearranged.

EDUCATIONAL GAMES FOR COMPUTERS

For the Apple II+ and IIe

Cause and effect / created by Learning Well.—Blue level ed., Version 1.1.—Roslyn Heights, N.Y. :Learning Well, c1982. 1 computer disk : col.

Crossword magic / by Larry Sherman.—Version 3.0.—Sunnyvale, CA : L & S Computerware, c1981.
  1 computer disk : double sides, col.

For the Commodore 64

Story machine.—Cambridge, MA : Spinnaker Software, c1983.
  1 computer cartridge : sd., col.

Selected Sources

Anglo-American Cataloguing Rules. 2nd ed. Chicago: American Library Association, 1978.

Dodd, Sue A. "Changing AACR2 to Accommodate the Cataloging of Microcomputer Software." *Library Resources & Technical Services* 29 (January/March 1985): 52.

"Free-floating Subdivisions." *Cataloging Service Bulletin,* Number 26 (Fall 1984), 36. "Computer programs" included as a free-floating subject heading.

Guidelines for Using AACR2 Chapter 9 for Cataloging Microcomputer Software. Chicago: American Library Association, 1984.

"International ISBN Agency: ISBN Software Numbering Scheme." *Library Hi Tech News* 1 (October-November 1984): 37. "Dr. Karl Neubauer, Director of the International ISBN Agency in Berlin, West Germany, notified all ISBN Agencies, in 42 countries worldwide to officially announce and confirm the 'inclusion of microcomputer software numbering within the scope of the ISBN system.' . . .More than five thousand microcomputer software publishers and producers have been assigned ISBN numbers for use on their software products.''

Selected Sources

Index

Accompanying material,3,5,6,7,9-10,16,19,21,32,36,38,49,
  52,54,57,59,61,63
   In simplified cataloging,67,68,69
Address given,5,16,21,29,36,39,44,47,52,54,57,59,61
  Not given,19,21,32,49,63
Age level,17,27,29,32,52
Anglo-American Cataloging Rules,1,14,71,75
Apple,19,27,29,32,36,38,49,54,57,61
   In simplified cataloging,68,69
Areas and their sources of information,2,3
Author entry,16,27,36,47,57
   In simplified cataloging,67,68
Back-up copies provided,63
Bank Street Writer,5,63
Based on other material,29,38
Basic books for remaining current,71-72
Bibliographies produced from catalog card information,72-73
Blank catalog card for mrdf,65-66
Book referenced in note,29,39
Business computer software,5,59-63
Calorimetry,36
Card 2,16-17,29-30,36,49
Cataloging Service Bulletin,1,14,71,75
Cause and Effect,5,54
Chem Lab Simulations,5,36
Chief source of information,1,4,60
Commodore 64,16,21,44,47,52,63
   In simplified cataloging,67,68
Commodore 64 Logo,4,21
   In simplified cataloging,68